Tidepool and Mangrove Shoals Murmurs

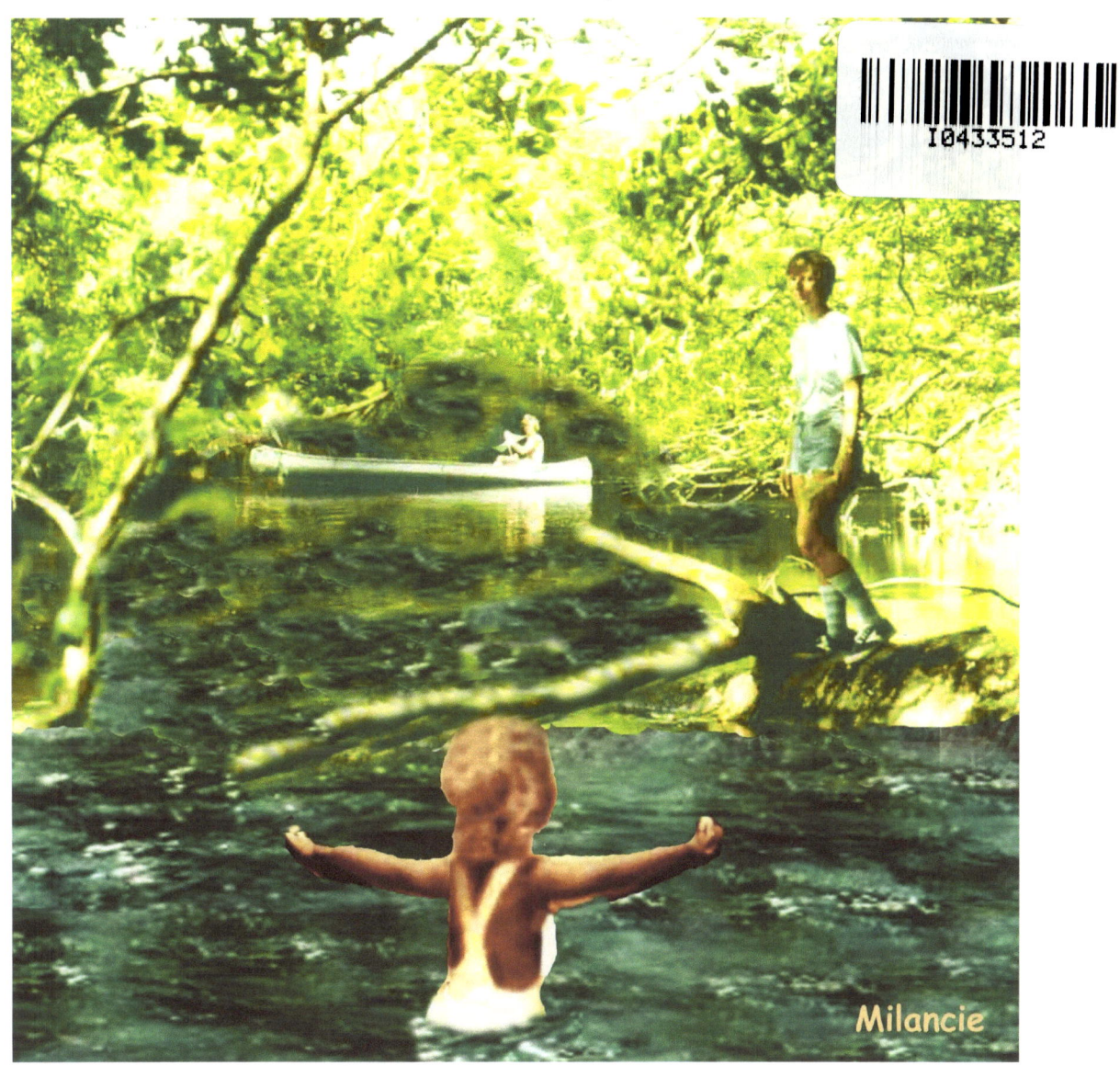

Milancie Hill Adams

Copyright © 2017 Milancie Hill Adams

All rights reserved.

ISBN-13: 978-1974309054 (CreateSpace-Assigned)
ISBN-10: 1974309053
LCCN: 2017912814
BISAC: Art / Subjects & Themes / Landscapes & Seascapes

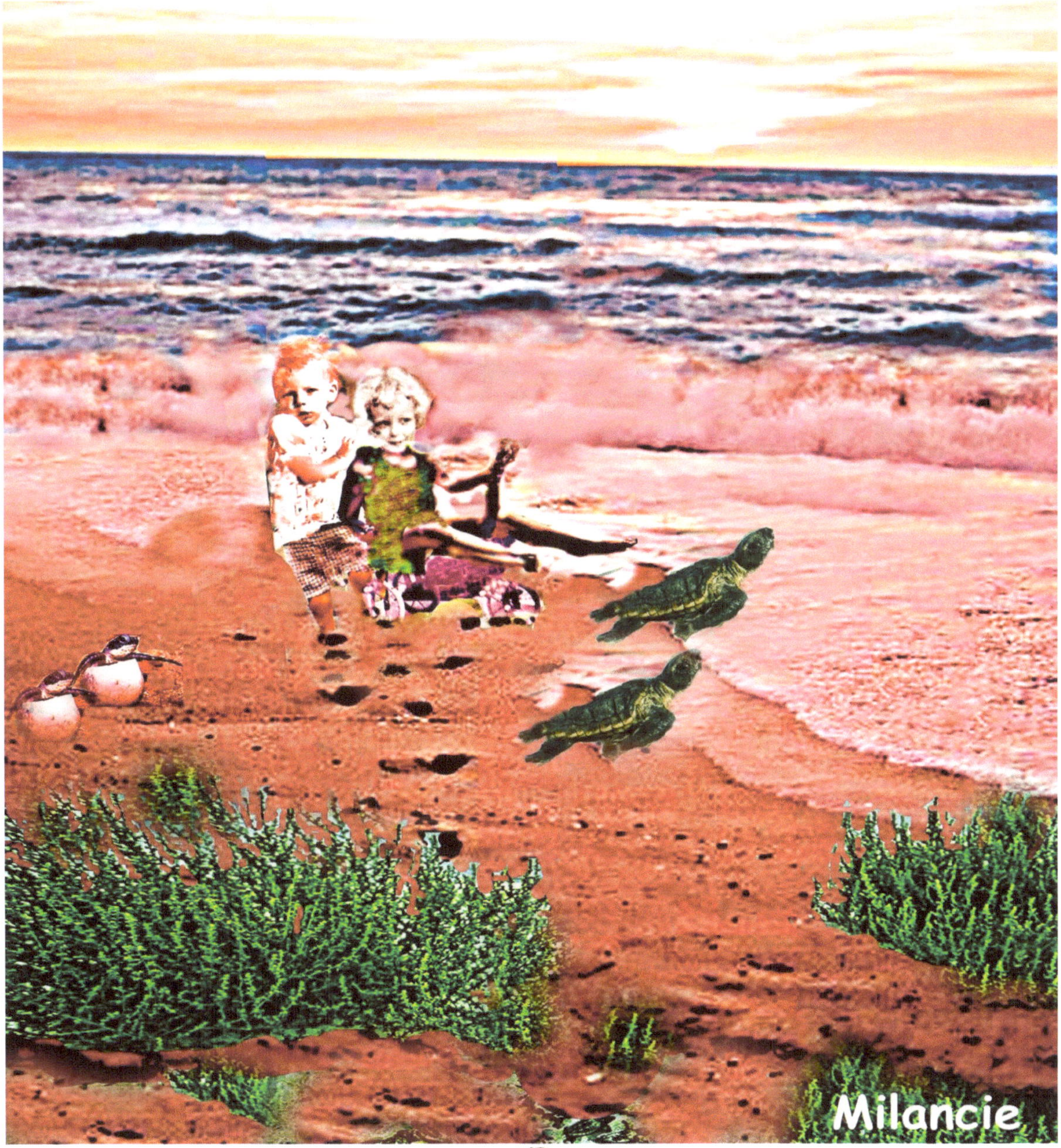

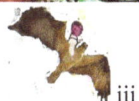

DEDICATION

This volume of Florida Illustrations and its poem is
dedicated to all those closest to me
who once circumvented with me
the beaches of Florida in awe
and now do so in Heaven's shoals
and to my close friend Mary Epifanio, her family
and my soulmate Alan Tietjen!

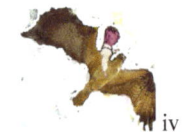

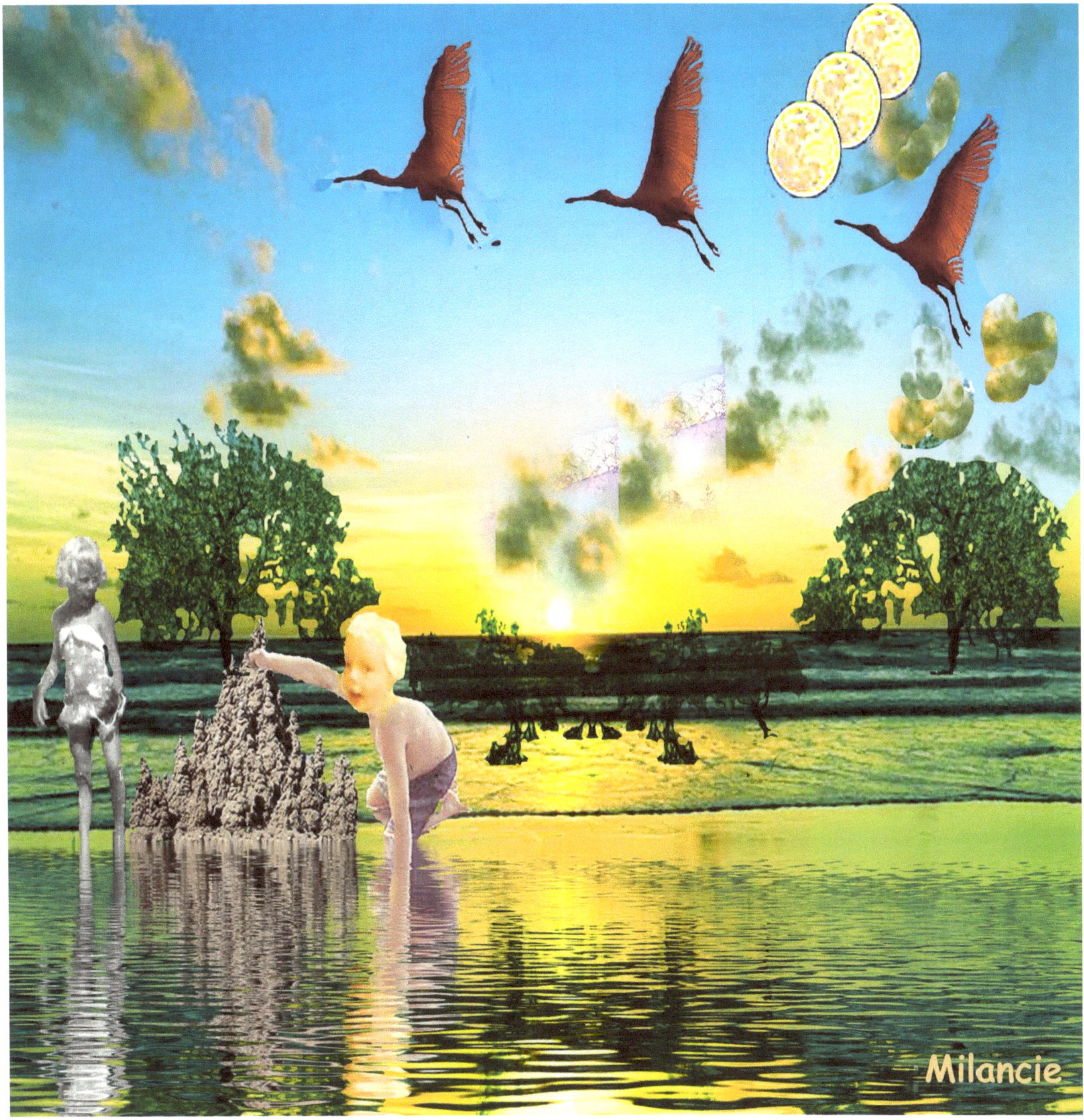

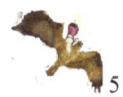

ACKNOWLEDGMENTS

My professors at FIT who did/do so much to preserve Florida waterways for future generations.

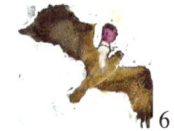

Memory of My Great Grandfather
(1833-1917)

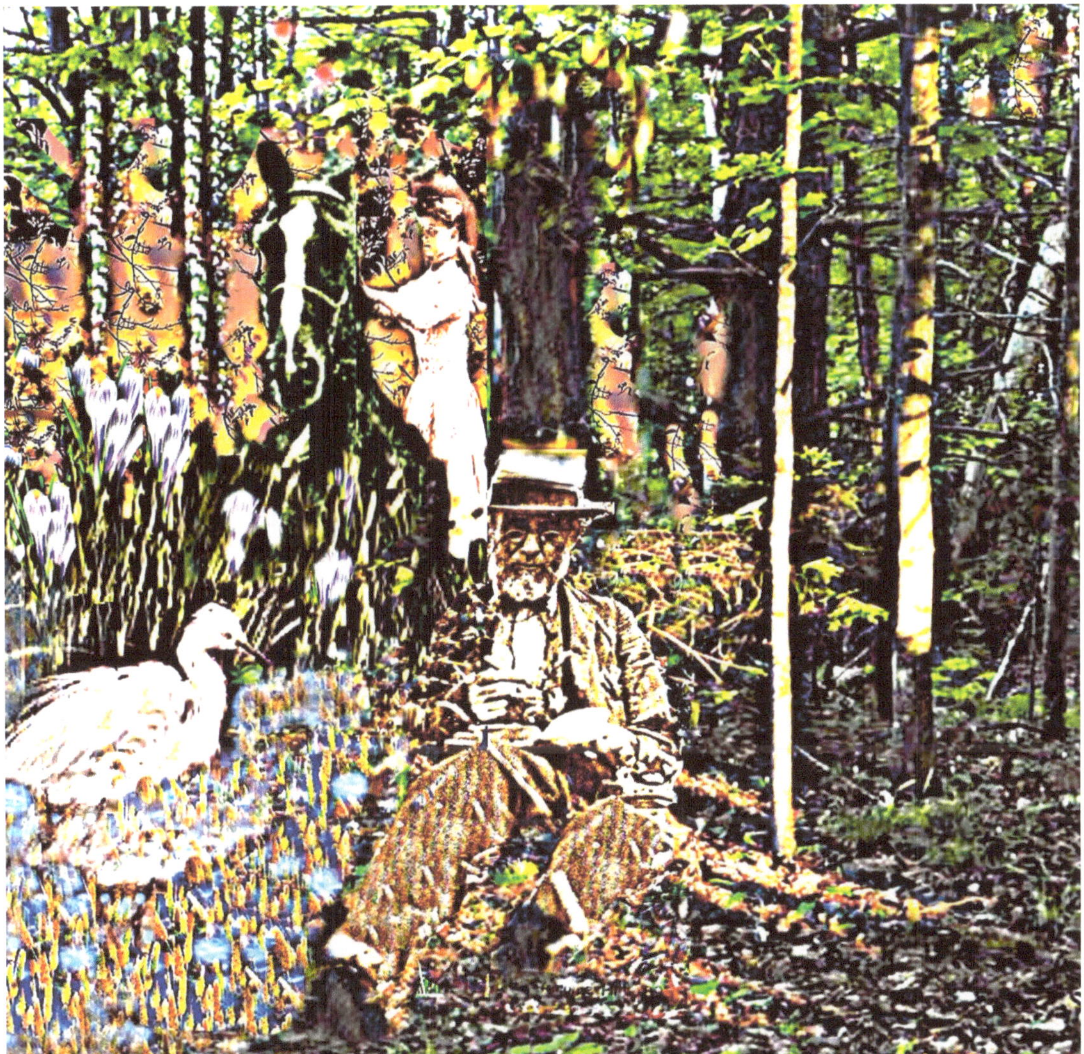

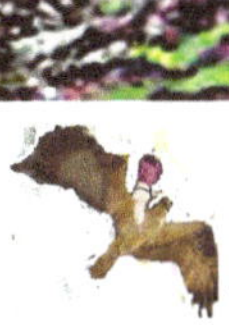

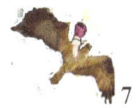

Ellsworth Jerome Hill, a self made man born in a log cabin, lame since childhood, was a Presbyterian minister, teacher and an American botanist. He conducted identifications and classifications of new American species. "In studying the flora of a restricted region, no matter how carefully it seems to have been explored, one is frequently surprised by new things.... No region can be regarded as thoroughly explored until every acre of its wild areas at least has been examined. Then some plants are so rare or local or grow under such peculiar conditions that a few square rods or even feet may comprise their range." - E.J. Hill, 1899

He amassed an herbarium of some 16,000 sheets, much the greater part being his own collections, and an exceptionally fine botanical library often frequenting sand barrens and swamps. He also left behind a manuscript detailing 133 species of mosses. The University of North Carolina Herbarium had, to date (2013), catalogued only half a dozen specimens collected by E.J. Hill. (www.herbarium.unc.edu/Collectors/Hill_Ellsworth.htm)

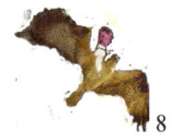

Introduction

Pitter Pat, pitter pat that's the sound of early morn or eve misty rain coming down. Sunlit browns and golden greens that's the smell of Florida's hammocks of moss laden mangrove islands, one of the last few outposts that remain untouched by over grown forests of beds now crowding a multitude of beaches.

Sunrise and sunset and since you are on an island there always a shoreline with a patch of sand to watch it from, you have just got to find it!

In these snarls of tangled greys and rusty sands with clusters of sea oats pulse gullies of warm waters snaking thru crevasses.

Darting here there and other the young play in these nurseries feeding on microorganisms sheltered by barnacles and oysters.

The islands are home to four species of mangrove, red, black, white and button wood. Their branches and trunks support various

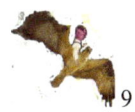

epiphytes, such as bromeliads including Spanish moss, and reindeer lichen. Below the water, spaces protected by splayed mangrove roots can shelter seagrasses.

"Ferns, vines, orchids, lilies, terns, herons, plovers, kingfishers, egrets, ibises, cormorants, snakes, lizards, spiders, insects, snails and mangrove crabs thrive on land or upper parts of the mangrove plants. Barnacles, oysters, mussels, sponges, worms, snails and small fish live around the roots."

"Mangrove forests provide vital habitat for endangered species from tigers and crocodiles to rare humming birds the size of a bee. Kennedy Ware wrote in National Geographic, "Forest mangroves form some of the most productive and biologically complex ecosystems on Earth. (factsanddetails.com/world/cat53/sub335/item2182.html)"

Growing up in Florida in the 50's in a small sleepy little beach town my grandmother, mother, sister, and I shared a large, rambling turn of the century two story coquina craftsman bungalow and its guesthouse overlooking the Halifax inland water way and only 10

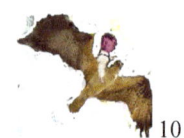

minutes from pristine beaches by bike over a wooden bridge.

Life for me began in the ocean with my mother, where she baptized me a water spirit at one month, immersing me in the waves.

When I took my first steps, it was barefoot on that beach, braving the wet foam and salty spray blowing off the waves' crests as the tides deposited glittering, fragile treasures in pools just beyond where I stood, transformed, as I squished cool wet sand with my toes. I had found my element!

As a graduate student I had the unique opportunity to study the mangrove ecosystem in person during a research trip to the Florida Keys.

What follows is an illustrated poem that served as my final paper for the class along with accompanying photographs I took. The photographs serve as backdrops for the poem's illustrations and its theme centering on the magical spiritual awe one can only encounter in these outposts still ignored by modern society.

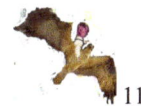

Nature beckoned
and I followed

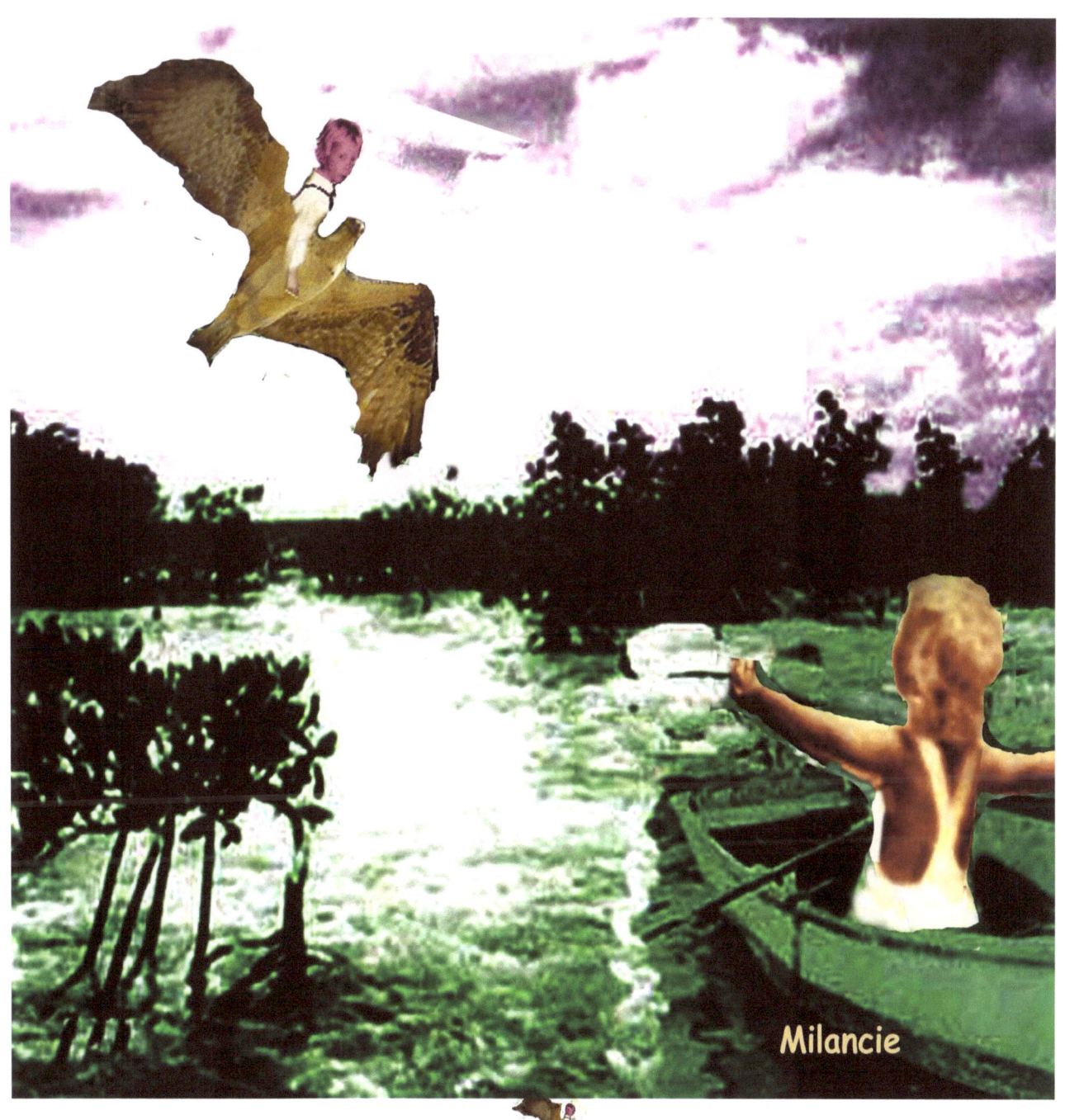

Circumventing the perimeter of beaches and shorelines

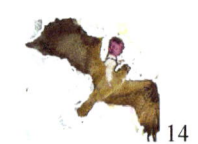

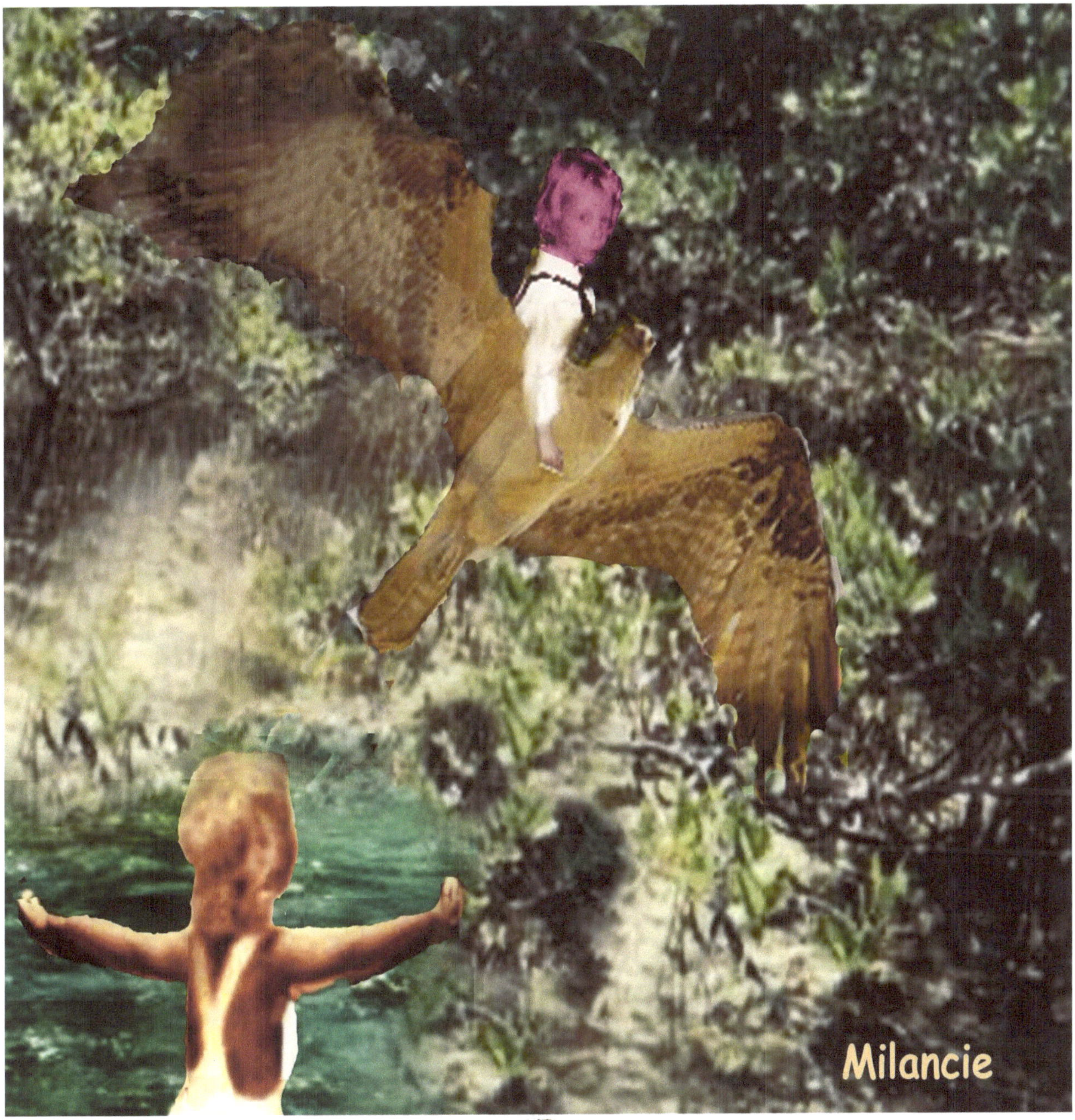

Milancie

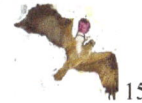

Down crevices and through channels

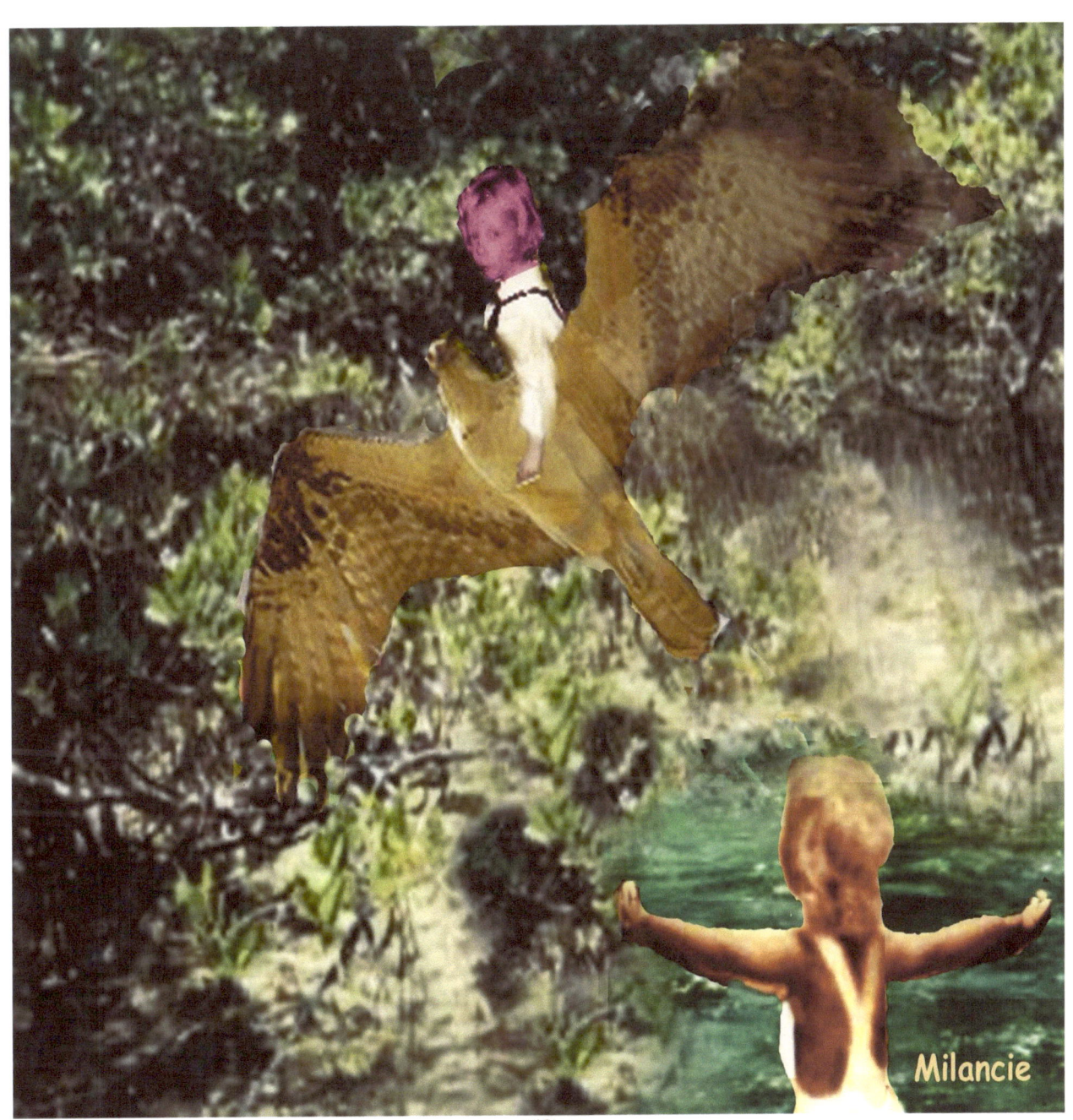

sometimes swimming, other times wading

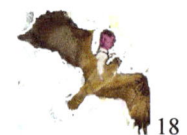

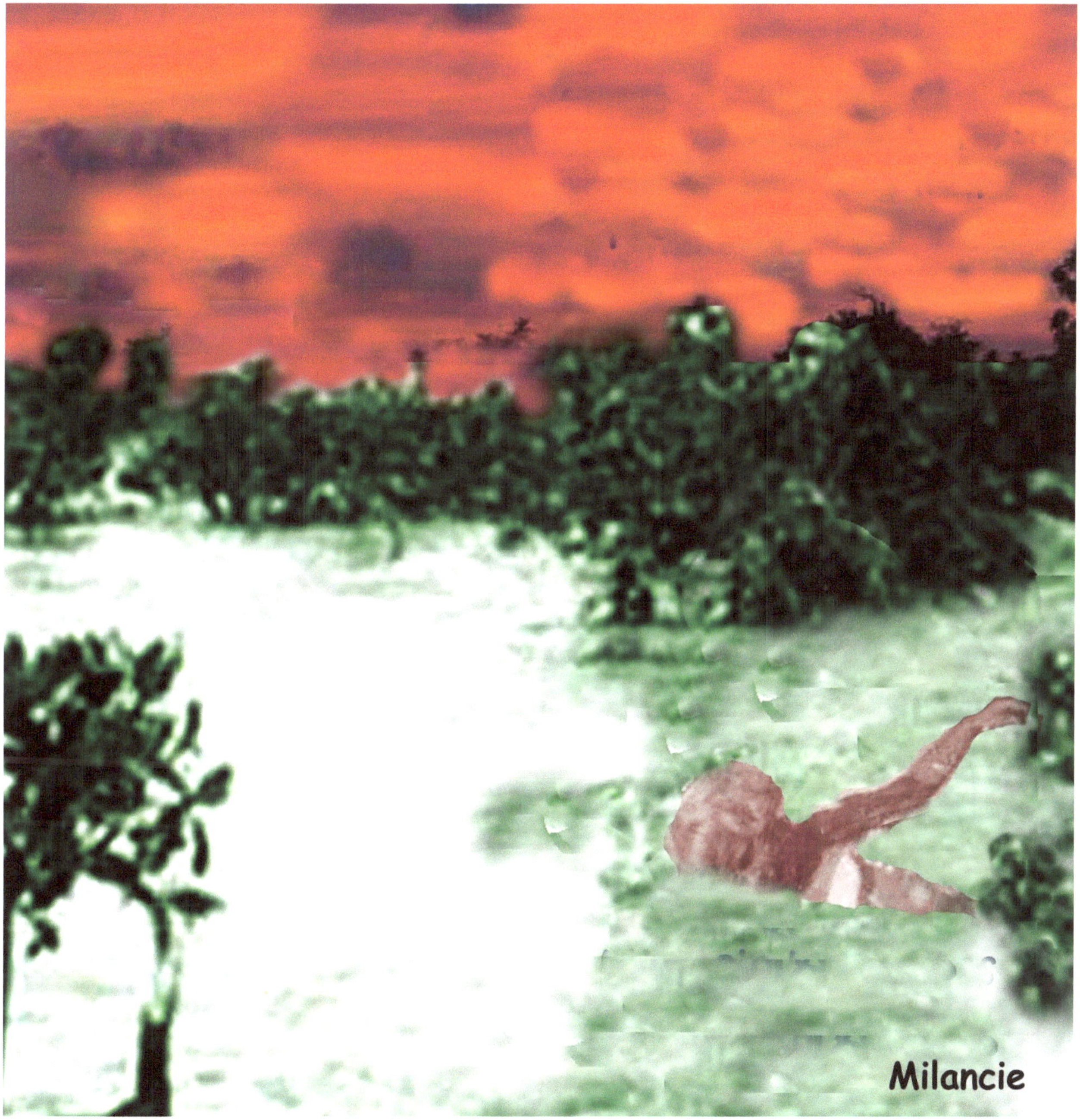

Milancie

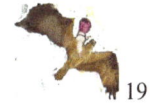

Looking and wandering, where I was being led

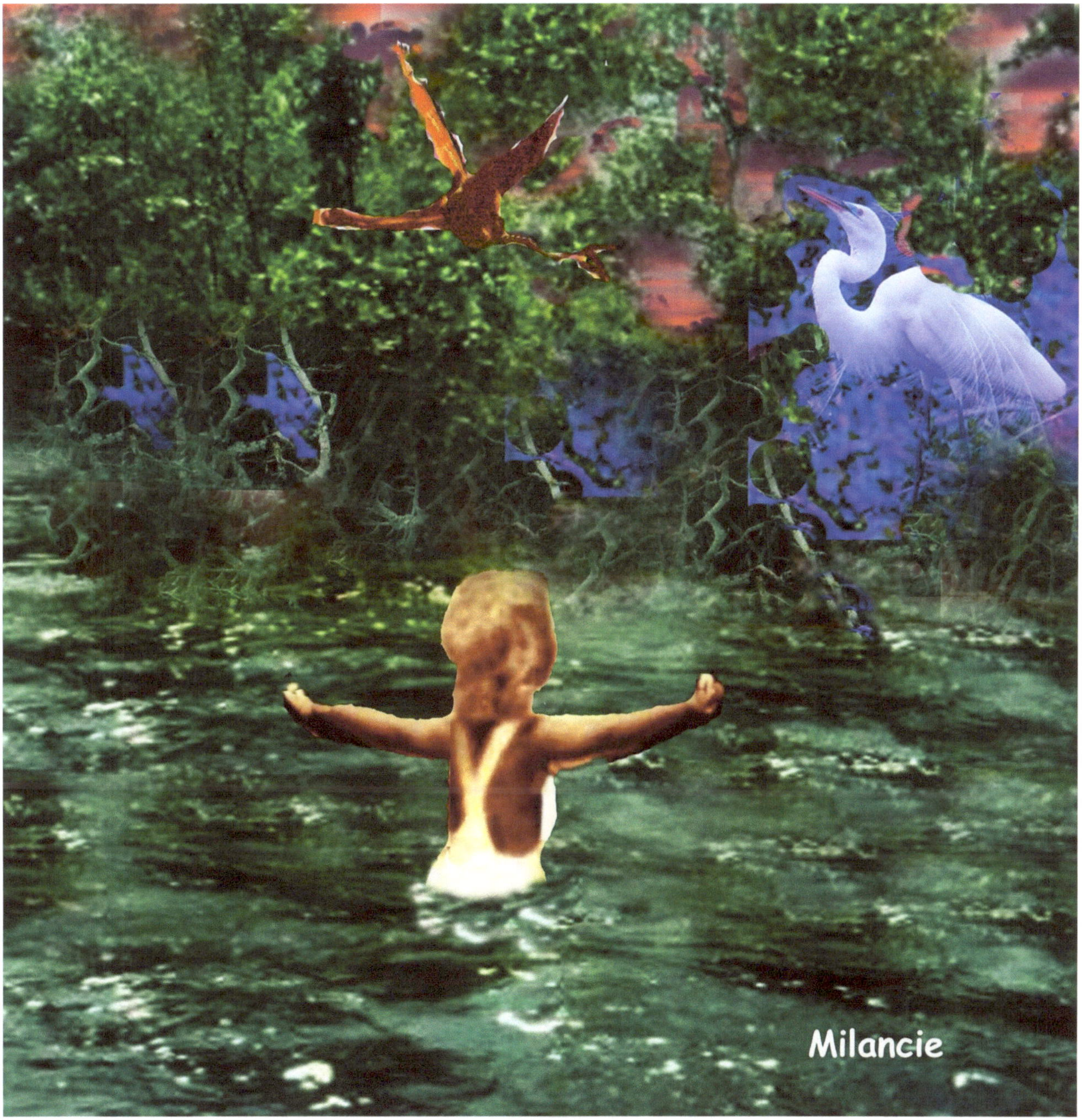

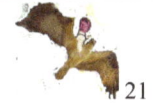

An osprey cried to its mate

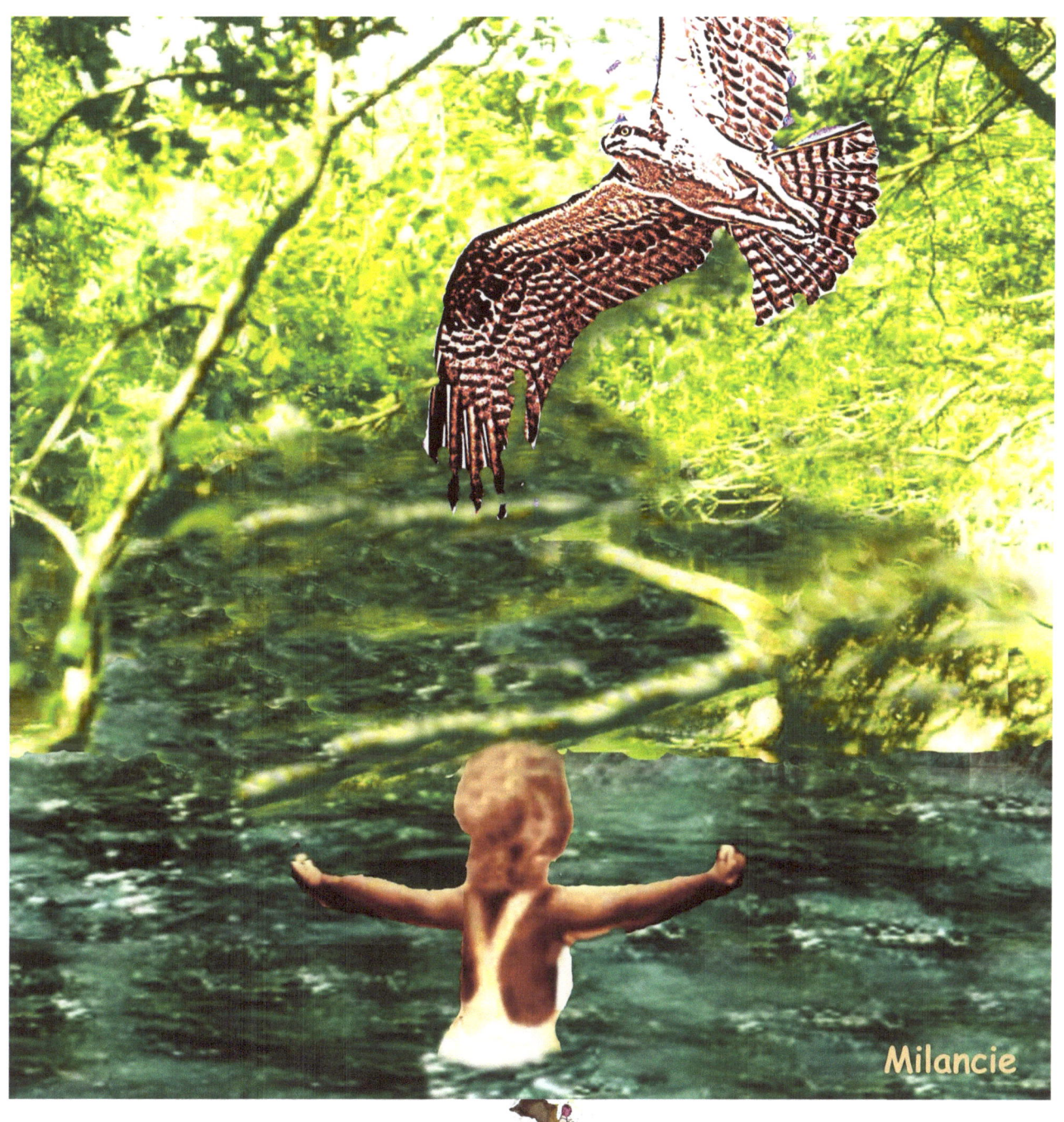

Its nest nestled above in the arms of an ancient mangrove

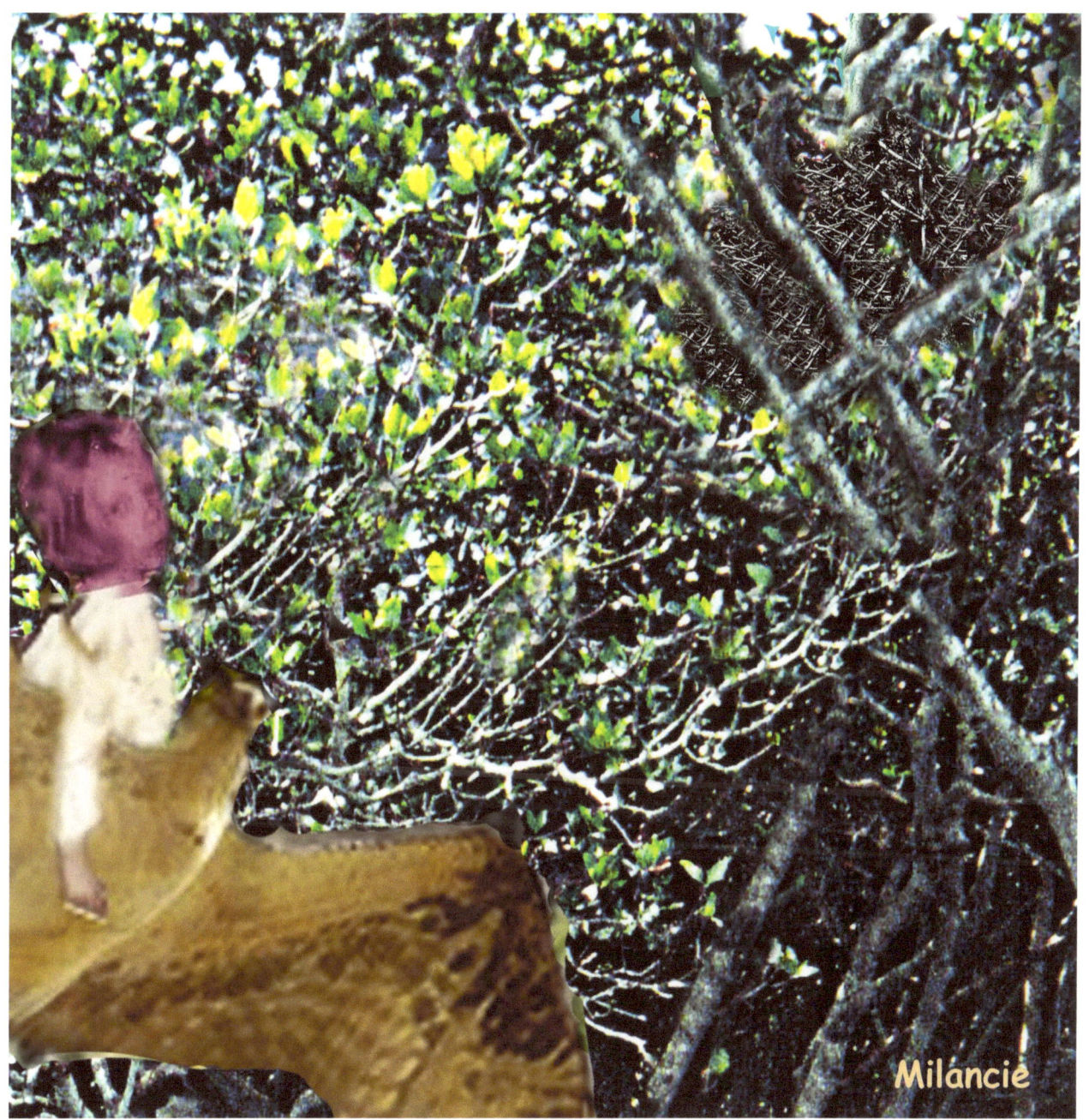

Littered below my feet
algae,
broken shells,
coral, and sponges

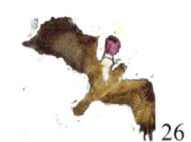

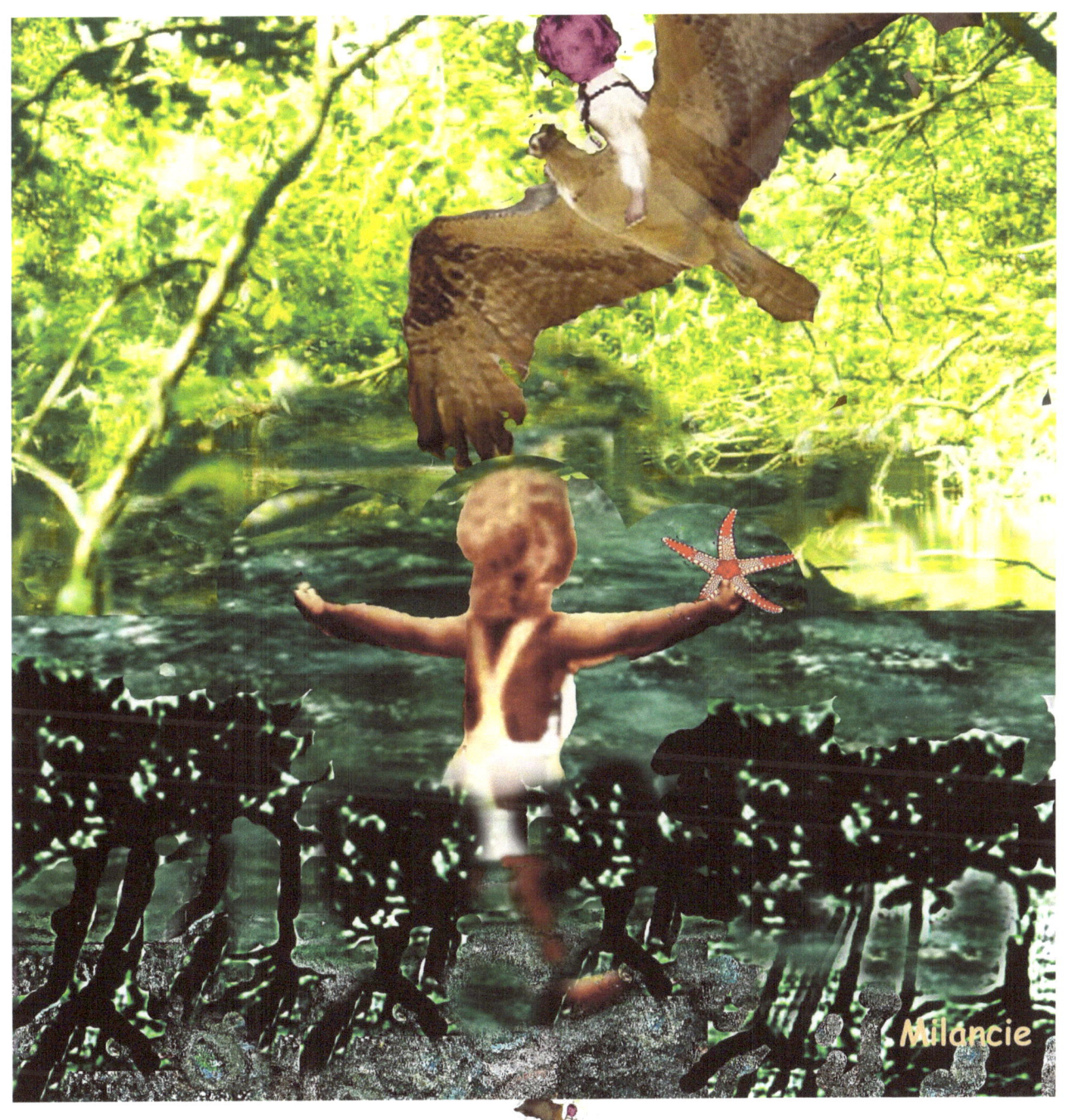

Overhead a crown pigeon rode the wind.

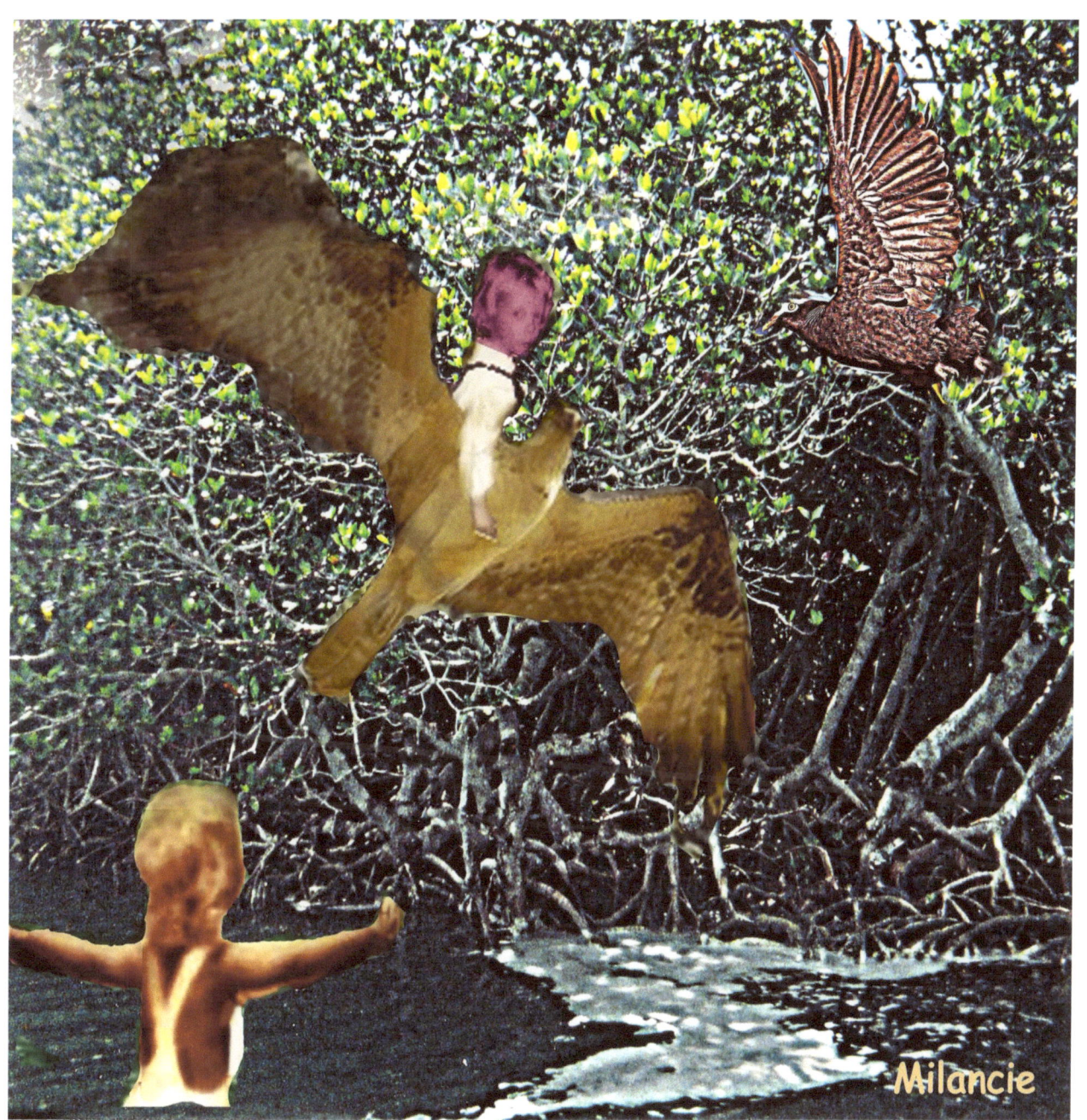

Now the currents picked up pulling me along

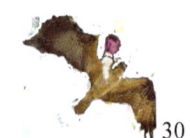

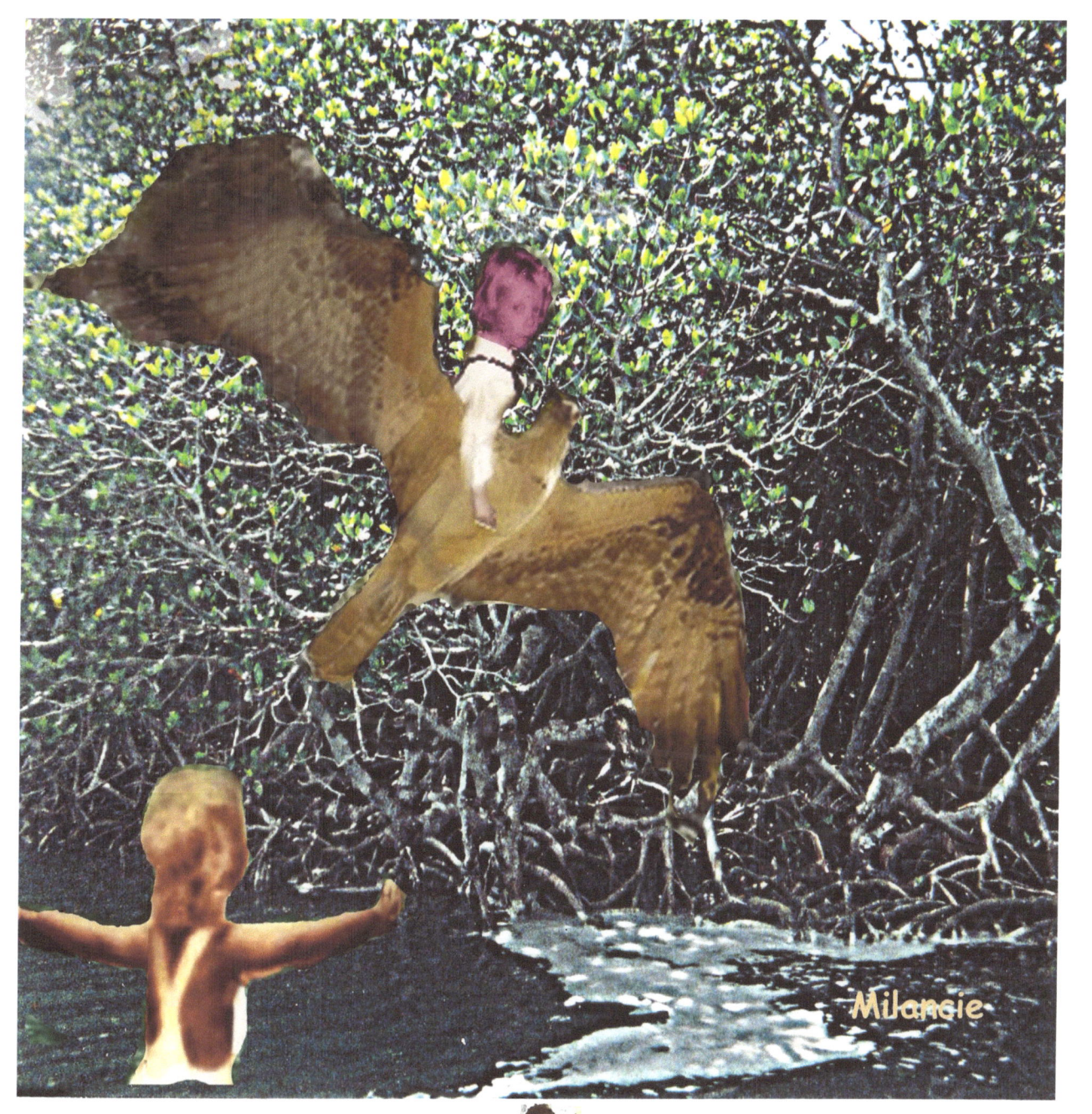

As if to say, don't tarry here too long

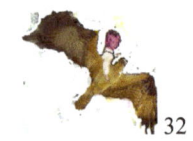

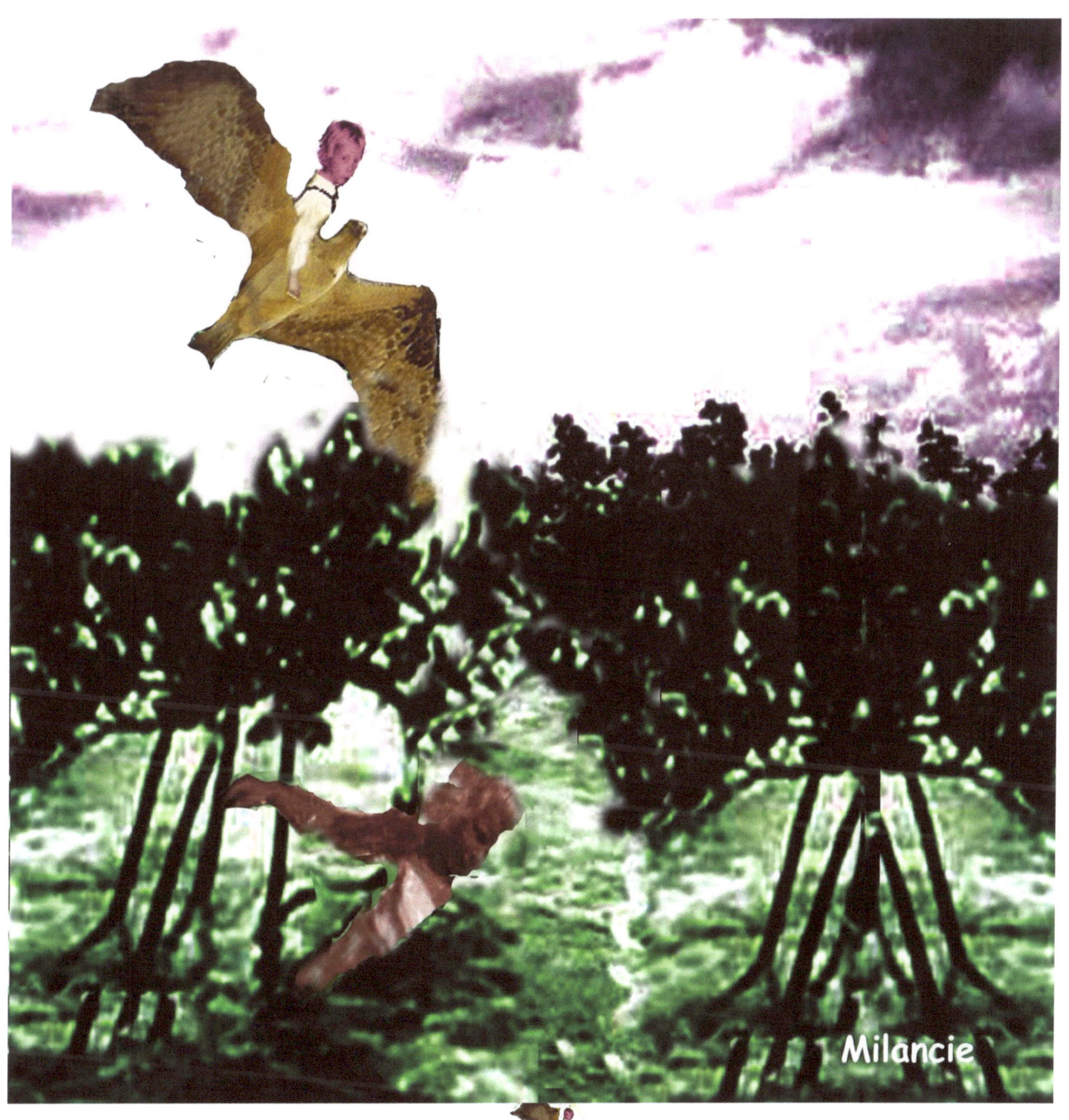

So much more to see,
still undisturbed by man
so little time!

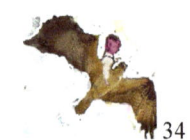

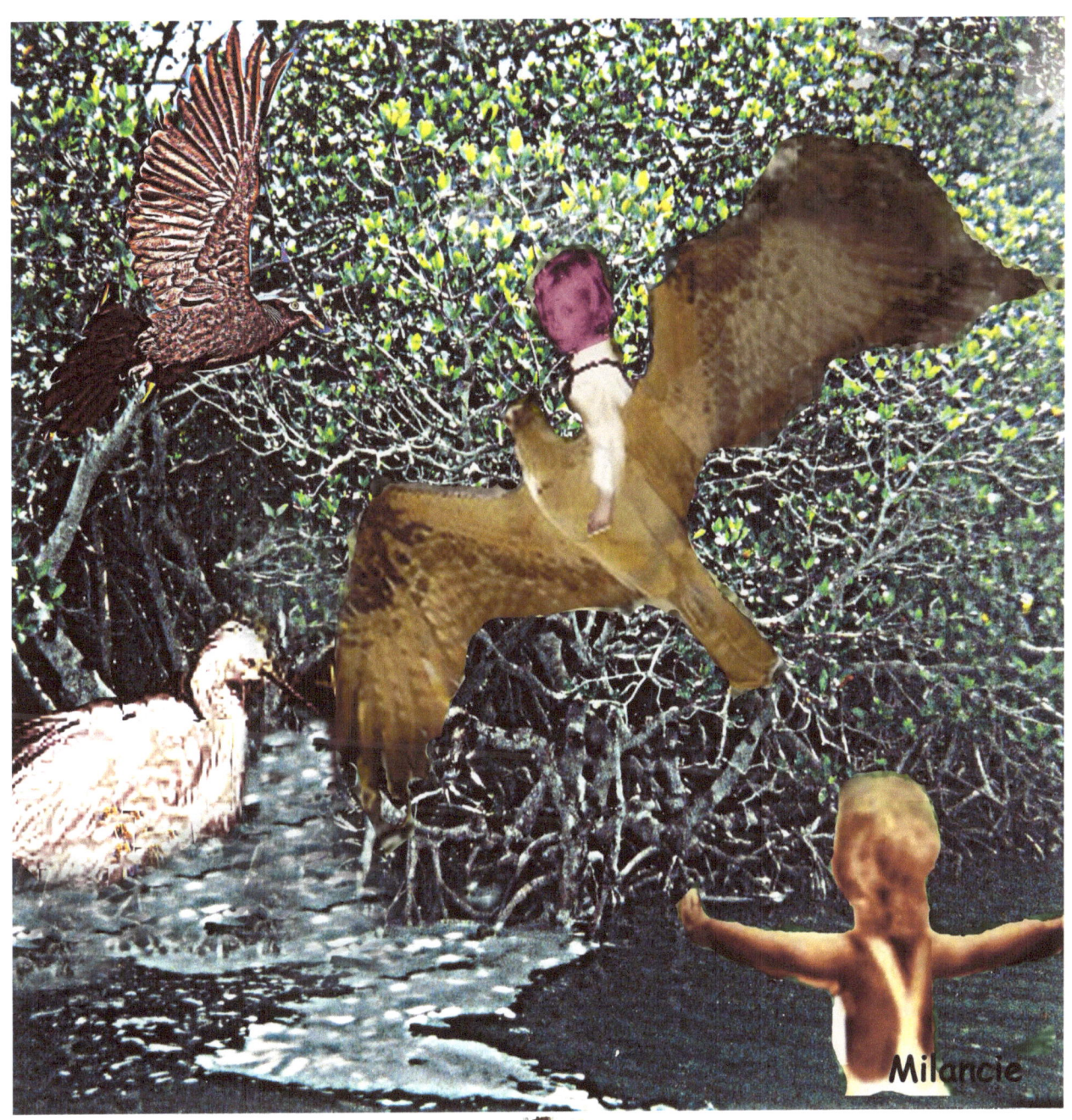

A nurse shark lurked nearby, in the roots, waiting and watching.

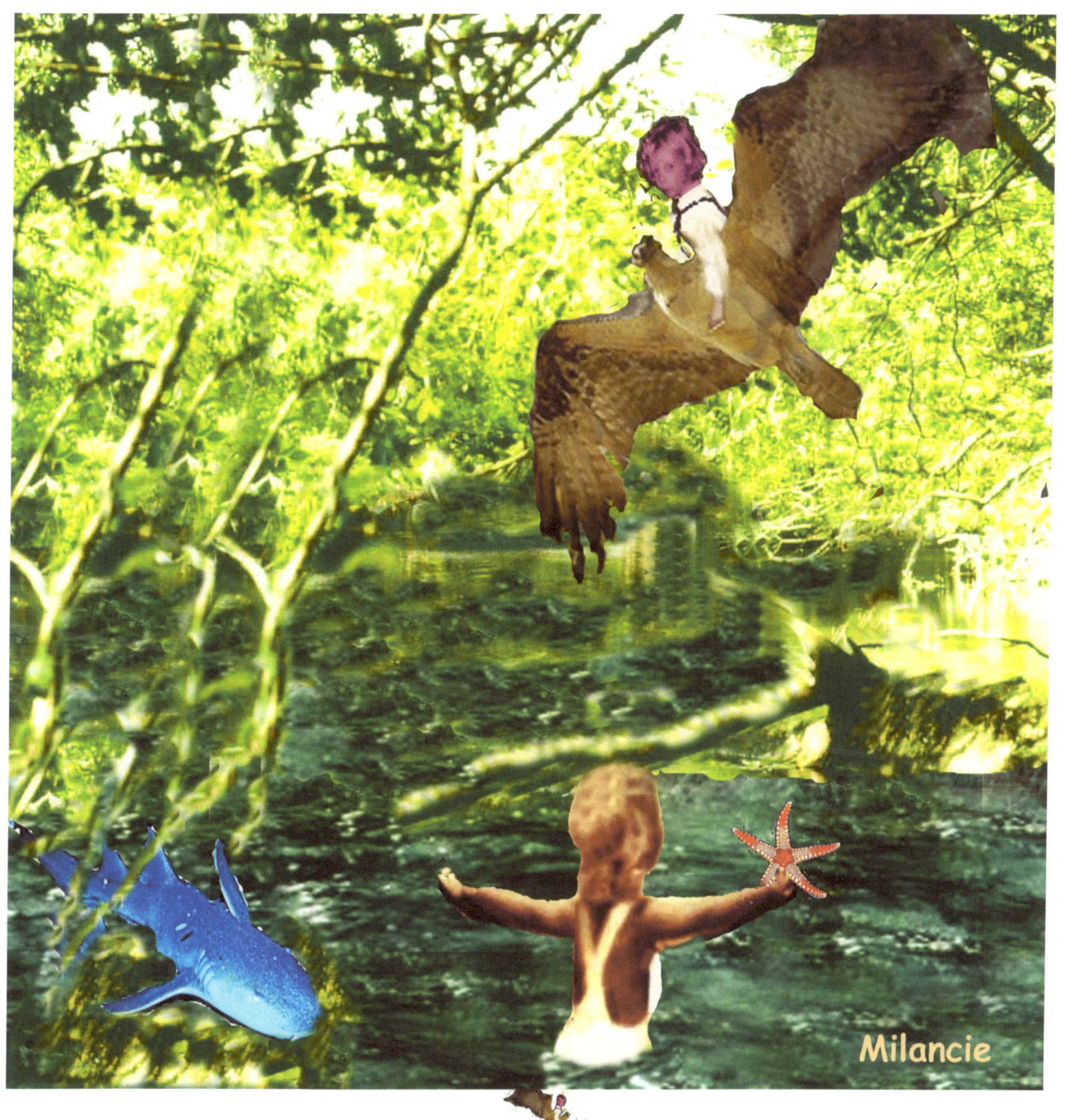

A sea ray raced by,

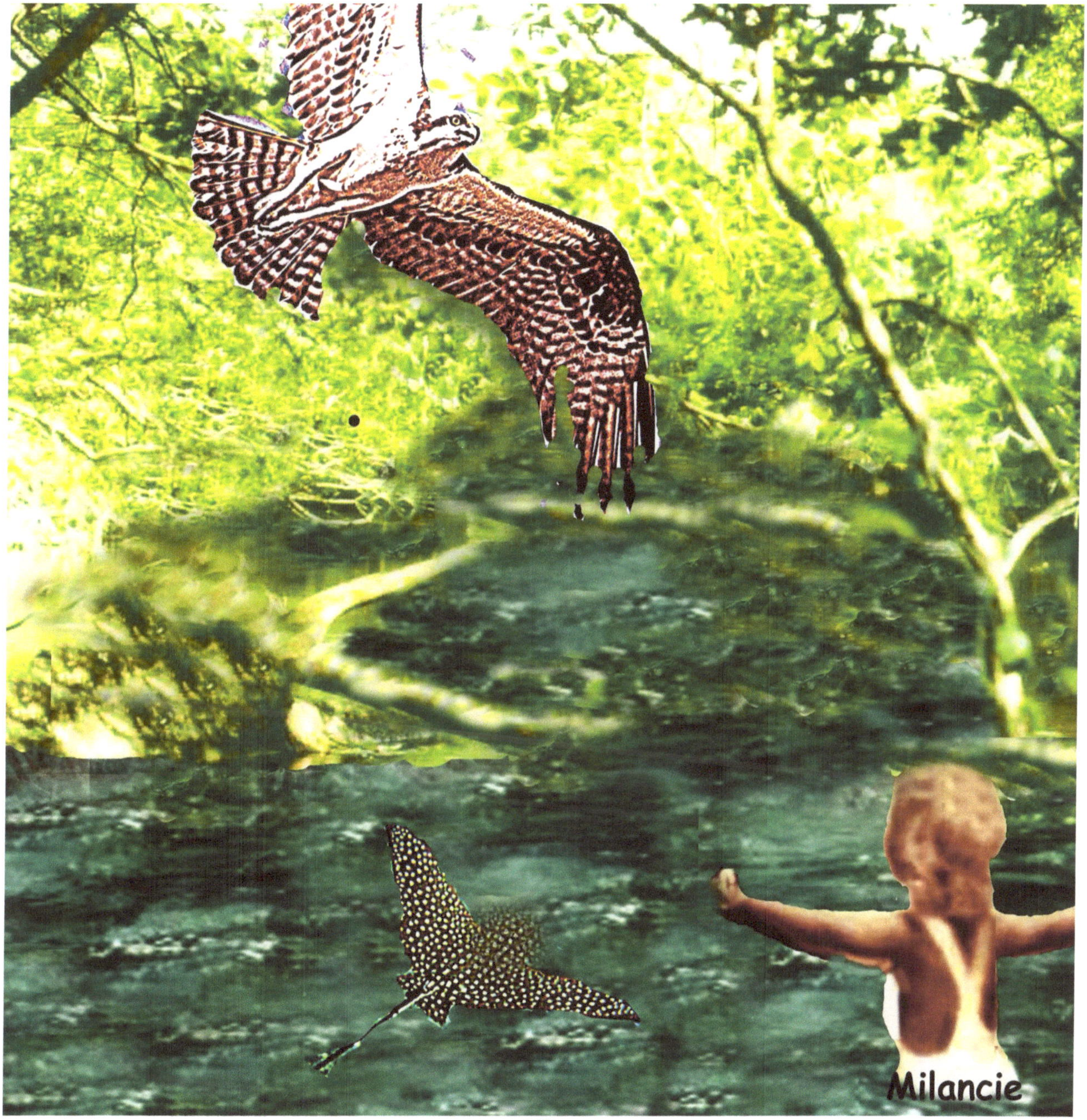

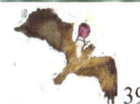

A starfish floated into my open hands

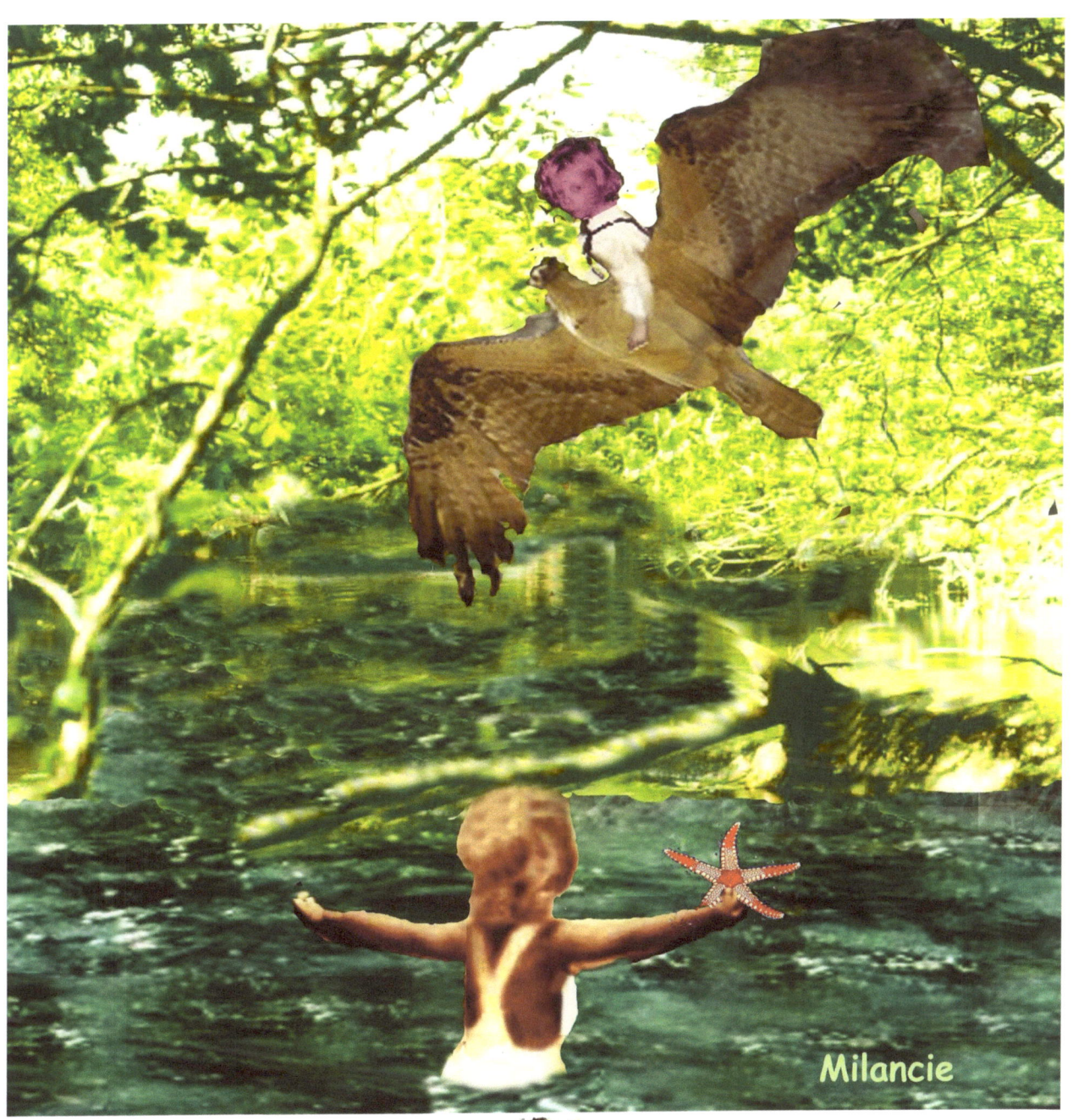

Below crabs danced and above gulls sailed

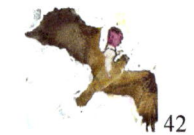

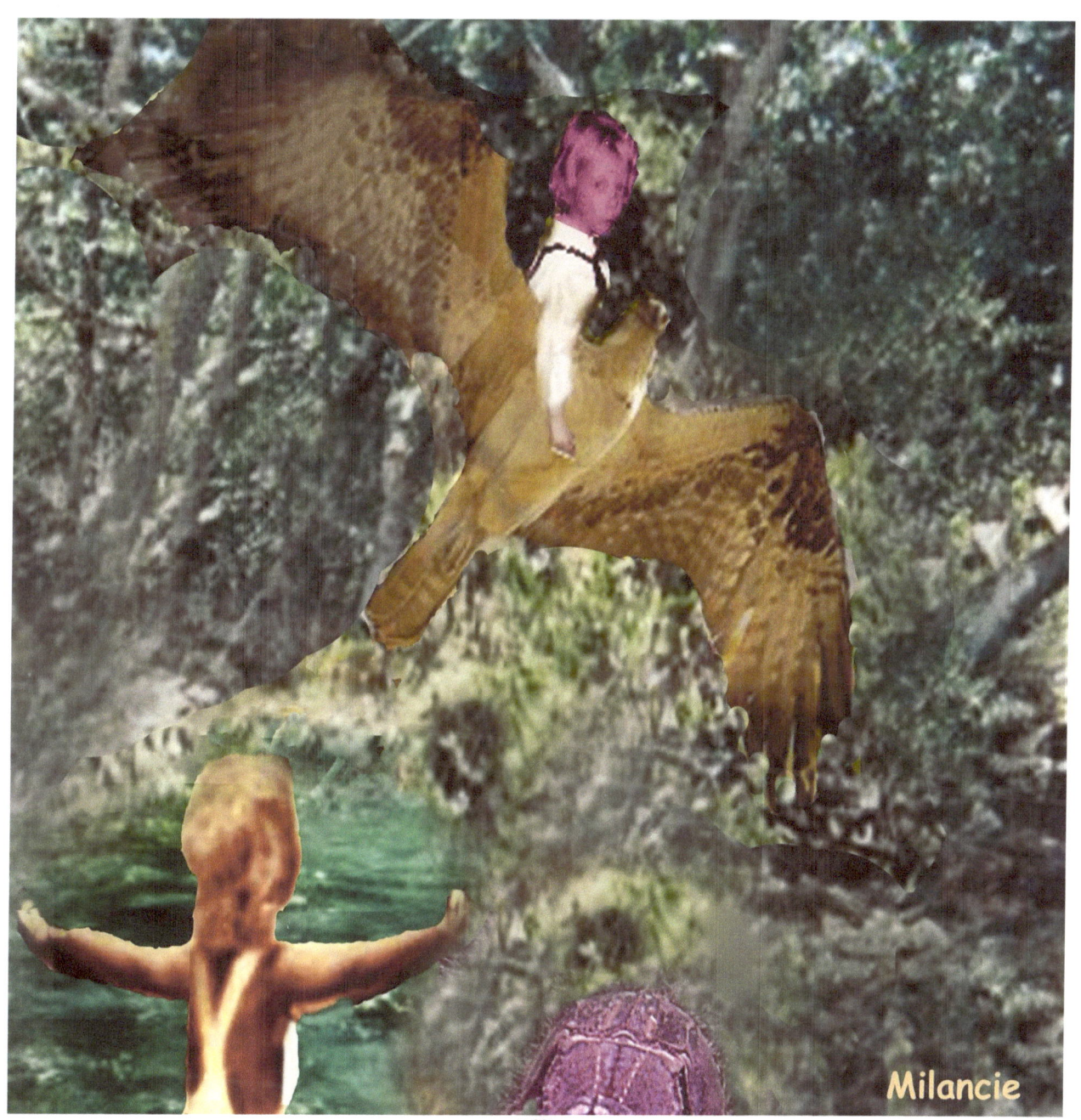

Then I knew! Nature beckoned me home

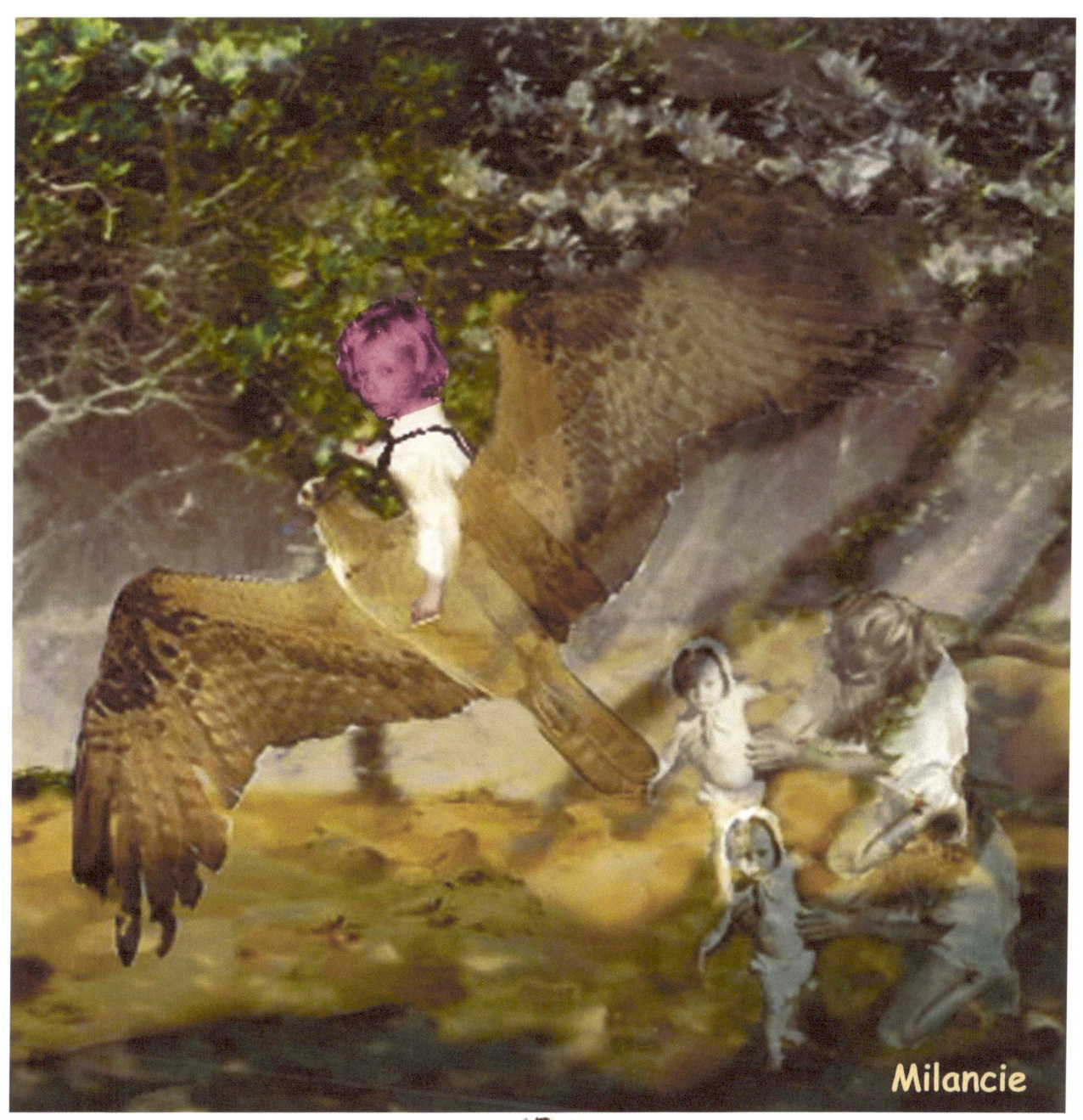
Milancie

and I followed back
to the Florida
of my childhood

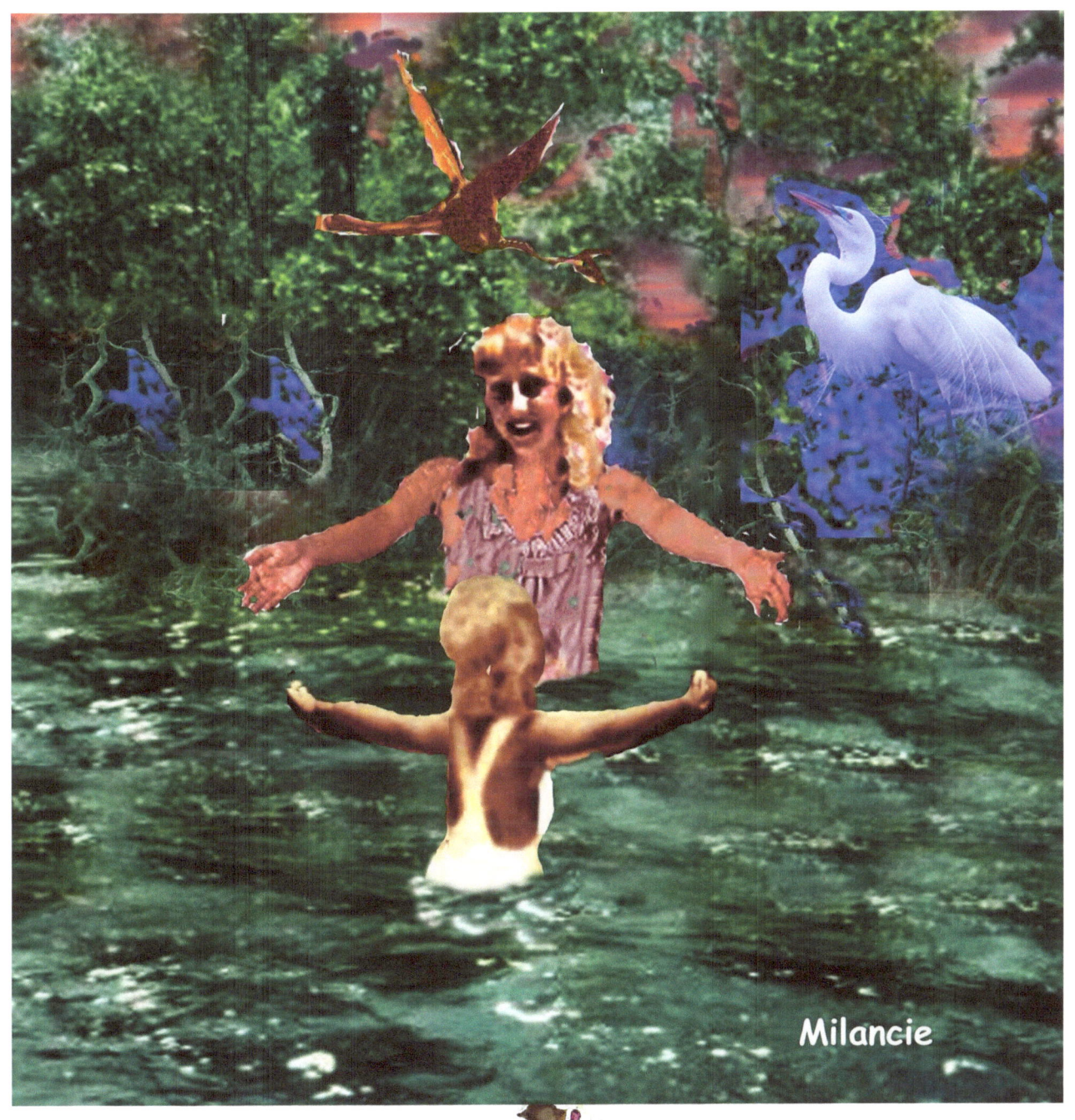

48

49

50

51

52

www.ingramcontent.com/pod-product-compliance
Lightning Source LLC
Chambersburg PA
CBHW051217220526
45473CB00003B/1063